Edition 2

Imprint: Independently published

i

2030 – When Computers become Human

"... what we found was that rather than being haphazardly arranged or independent pathways, we find that all of the pathways of the brain taken together fit together in a single exceedingly simple structure. They basically look like a cube. They basically run in three perpendicular directions, and in each one of those three directions, the pathways are highly parallel to each other and arranged in arrays. So, instead of independent spaghettis, we see that the connectivity of the brain is, in a sense, a single coherent structure."

Van J. Wedeen, a Harvard neuroscientist and physicist.

A study at the Massachusetts General Hospital

Funded by the National Institutes of Health, March 2012.

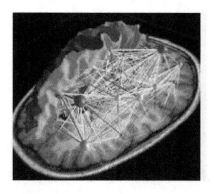

2030 – When Computers become Human

ACKNOWLEDGEMENTS

I'D LIKE TO EXPRESS MY GRATITUDE TO THE FOLLOWING PEOPLE WHO PROVIDED ME WITH KNOWLEDGE, INSPIRATION AND THE VISION TO WRITE THIS BOOK.

They are:

Ray Kurzweil, futurist, author, inventor and visionary. His book, **The Singularity is Near**, inspired me to write this book. He helped me understand the relationship between the computer and human intelligence, and his research publications exposed me to advances in artificial intelligence and voice recognition.

Phil Savenick, author, artist, director, and filmmaker. I was honored to visit his home which features a museum of television history, and a shrine to Philo Farnworth, the inventor of television. He helped me understand the intimate relationship between computer monitors and television.

2030 – When Computers become Human

TABLE OF CONTENTS

2030 – When Computers become Human

PROLOGUE

Where did counting begin? Artifacts more than 5,000 years old have been found, with notches on bones. Were these notations etched as a means of counting seasons, kills, or children?

The origins of mathematics accompanied the evolution of social systems. All basic social needs require calculation and numbers. As society formed and organized, the need to express quantity emerged.

When society emerged from hunting and gathering to an agrarian society, there was a need to account for food on hand as well as surpluses. Counting probably arose spontaneously more or less independently from place to place, and tribe to tribe. Various numbering systems arose, all remarkably similar.

2030 – When Computers become Human

The transition from counting with markers to counting with mechanical devices occurred over thousands of years. Then society realized that records of accounting were required, and statistics were saved and archived. Scientists came along and developed logic to accompany counting, and math and the early computer were born.

Alan Turing
OBE, FRS

Who first conceived of the idea that someday computers would "think" in ways that one could not distinguish a computer from a human? Perhaps it was **Alan Turing**. Born in 1912, this British mathematician, cryptanalyst *(in World War II)*, computer scientist and marathon runner designed and developed the **Turing Machine**, which was the first model of a general-purpose computer.

2030 – When Computers become Human

More germane to this book is Turing's prediction that computers would someday "think" so similarly to humans, that if a problem was posed to a human in one room, and a computer in another, the questioner could not distinguish from which room the answer came from. He predicted that this would happen within 50 years with a 30% success rate. Although his prediction did not materialize, recent breakthroughs in artificial intelligence indicate that, by 2030, the 30% "indistinguishable" rate will be achieved or exceeded.

PART I. EVOLUTION

Counting and Numbers

Before 1800, little was known about "computing" other than the use of counting devices dating back to the ancient abacus. In 1804, Frances Jacquard developed a fully automated loom that was programmed by an early version of the punch card. By 1820, Charles Xavier Thomas de Colmar created the "Arithometer", the first commercially successful calculating machine, which remarkably could add, subtract, multiply and divide.

In parallel with the stages of development of the computer was the evolution of number systems. It all started when humans had reasons to count. Animals count their young, and birds desert their nests when more than one egg is taken from them.

Ancient Incas, a highly advanced civilization, had no written language but developed the Quipu counting system, a system where thin strings were looped around a larger cord. It is believed that this was the first base-10 numbering system.

2030 – When Computers become Human

Ancient Egyptians developed the concept of fractions. They wrote fractions with a numerator of 1 but used hieroglyphics for the denominator. Their numbering system was a base-10 system with a unique sign for every power of 10.

The Babylonian system is one of the oldest number systems, dating back 5,000 years. It was a system of wedge-shaped "tally" marks, and had a value depending upon the direction in which the wedge was pointing. It was also the first symbolic system used to tell time of day.

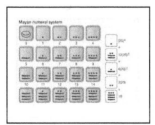

The Mayan numbering system in the fourth century was perhaps a thousand times more advanced than the European system. They used a Base-20 system which had only two symbols, a dot and a dash. They were the first to symbolize the concept of zero.

2030 – When Computers become Human

The Greek numbering system, interestingly enough, was based upon their alphabet, which came from the Phoenicians.

The Roman numbering system, still used today, had a rather static numbering system which change only slightly through time. It is perhaps best known in the United States for counting Super Bowls, and universally for the copyright date on films, on watch faces and clocks, and for succession of religious leaders such as Popes.

The base-10 decimal system is the most widely used system in the civilized world. Because it uses the digits 0 through 9 and powers of ten for the position of the digit in the number, it can represent any number, no matter how large.

However, the decimal system does not lend itself to logical processes, nor can it easily be integrated on a computer's processor *(or chip)*. However, the binary system, which is a base-2 system that uses two symbols, 0 and 1, called "bits", can represent logic as well, where 1 is true and 0 is false.

2030 – When Computers become Human

All data and logical operations within a computer's memory or processor is stored as a series of zeros and ones. The position of a bit within a sequence of bits has a value based upon the power of 2. For example, the four bits represented by "0111" has a decimal value of 14 (0+2+4+8). Arabic characters and numbers are represented in 8 bits, and can be displayed as a Hexadecimal number represented by the digits 0-9 followed by the characters A-F. For example, the decimal number 15 is stored in a computer in the hexadecimal system as an "**E**" which is stored in the computer as binary "1111".

Computer commands at the lowest level in Assembly Language are represented by two hexadecimal characters; for example, the Branch on Condition command is "**FC**". More about this in chapter I-8. Programming Languages on page 20.

The Babbage Engine

Charles Babbage was born on December 26th, 1791, the son of a banker. He graduated from Cambridge University in 1810, and always possessed a keen interest in mathematics and an awesome knowledge of calculus.

Often called "The Father of Computing," Babbage was an innovative thinker and a pioneer in the computing field. His knowledge of mathematics was so respected that he was hired by the Royal Institution shortly after graduation to lecture on calculus. Only two years later, he was elected a member of the Royal Society and along with his associates, founded the Astronomical Society in 1820.

In 1822, Babbage designed a "difference engine", which is a mechanical calculator which tabulates polynomial functions. The engine itself consists of parallel tubular columns which must be precisely machined so that they produce error-free calculations. This machine used the decimal number system and was powered by cranking a handle.

2030 – When Computers become Human

The British government became most interested in Babbage's engine, since producing tables of statistics was time-consuming, costly, and not always 100% accurate.

In 1822, Babbage presented a "difference engine" to the Royal Astronomical Society in a paper entitled *"Notes on the application of machinery to the computation of astronomical and mathematical tables."* The British government gave Babbage £1700 and work on the project began.

Babbage's goal was to overcome errors in tables through mechanization. Every part of the engine had to be formed by hand using custom machine tools, which Babbage constructed.

The result was an engine that was able to calculate polynomials by using a numerical method called the "differences" method. His first engine, completed in 1822, produced discrepancies but was far more accurate than earlier mechanical devices.

2030 – When Computers become Human

In 1832, Babbage published **On the Economy of Machinery and Manufactures**, which influenced early work on operations research, a method for improving the structure for industrial production and the division of labor.

Babbage is considered to be the eminent pioneer in computing, having developed the first mechanical computer and, later on, more accurate steam-powered machines that mechanized calculations of polynomials.

Boolean Logic

 **George Boole**, born in 1815, was an English mathematician, philosopher and logician. He is considered to be the inventor of Boolean Logic, which is the foundation of the digital computer.

In 1849, Boole was appointed as the first professor of mathematics at Queens College in Ireland. His early works attempted to systematize the fundamental principles of Aristotle's logic.

Boole did not regard logic as a branch of mathematics. Instead, he proposed that logical propositions could be presented algebraically through the manipulation of symbols in equations.

The fundamental thesis for his logic consists of "elective symbols", primarily the logical operators "and" and "or" (represent in formulas as "**&**" and "**|**"). This, coupled with a base numbering system with the lowest level a 1 or a 0, is the essence of Boolean logic in algebraic equations. Boole is no doubt the inventor of computer

2030 – When Computers become Human

programming, which is discussed further in I-8. Programming Languages on page 37.

Boole's contributions to the algebra in logic were viewed as immensely important and influential in the development of computer processors.

In early computers the Central Processing Unit (CPU) hosted this algebraic logic, basic commands and mathematical operations, which was in essence the composite of a computer program.

Boole also conceived of the fundamental method of comparing "sets" by using just three operators: AND (**&**), OR (**|**) and NOT (**¬**).

His novel approach of using only two symbols (1 and 0) to represent opposites is fundamental in programming logic. Tests of the symbols to mean "yes-no", "true-false" or "on-off" can result in "branches" to a portion of a program depending on whether it is a 1 or a 0. Furthermore, these tests can be nested within other tests and resolved from the inside out to produce a single "true" or "false".

Boolean logic is not only used in computer software *(programs)* but also in computer hardware. In essence, various "Gates" on a chip will affect the flow and direction through a computer program.

Gates are the logical "switching stations" on any computer. But what is a "computer"? The fundamental architectural model of a computer was first described in June 1945 by **John von Neumann** and it survives today.

The von Neumann model states that a computer consists of (1) a central processing unit (CPU), (2) an arithmetical and logical component (ALU), (3) mass storage, (4) a program "counter", and (5) input / output (I/O) channels. It has been

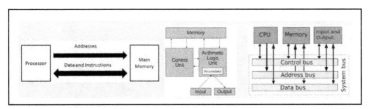

the "bible" for computer engineers and designers.

In 1935 von Neumann introduced the concept of a stored program which could be stored in random access memory (RAM). Charles Babbage's Analytical Engine incorporated the von Neumann model and provided the ability to input

2030 – When Computers become Human

a computer program from a deck of punch cards, a concept based upon the Jacquard loom of 1801.

von Neumann was probably the first to articulate the similarity between a computer and a brain. The output of neurons in the brain is essentially digital and sequential, but massively parallel processes exist that will ultimately achieve the "singularity[1]" between the brain and the computer. Neural output is embedded in an axon in the brain, which is remarkably similar to an analog signal. Processing in dendrite "sensors" are input to the neuron.

---

[1] Ray Kurzweil. The Singularity is Near (2005).

Hollerith's Punch Card System

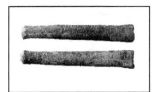

Throughout history, civilized man has had a need to record information. The first evidence of the use of the number 1 seems to be about 20,000 years ago, when a uniform series of single lines were cut into the "Ishanga" bone *(the fibula of a baboon)* discovered by archaeologists.

Numbers and counting did not come into extensive use until the rise of cities and commerce, around 4000 BC. When subtraction joined addition, arithmetic was born.

Evidence of recording devices can be seen in clay cones that were stored in pouches. Later, these cones were replaced by marks on clay tablets. Ancient Sumerians recognized the need for people to keep track of "things", and the first accountants went to work.

2030 – When Computers become Human

Around 3000 BC the number 1 transitioned from a counting unit to a unit of measurement. Builders of temples and pyramids invented the cubit, the first standardized unit for measurement, about 17.5 inches.

Under the guidance of Pythagoras, the Greeks developed the concept of odd and even numbers. Later, another Greek mathematician Archimedes conceived theoretical math, and his experimentation with math games led to practical application in the world of commerce and banking.

When counting and calculating with numbers, one needs to store that data so that it can be recalled later from archives, or analyzed by accountants, researchers or census bureaus. Politicians need to know how many constituents are in their district, and whether they are red or blue.

The earliest medium for data storage in early PCs was in the form of "punch cards" containing at first, round holes and later, rectangular holes which sometimes had hanging chads, made infamous in the 2000 Florida election recount. One of the early uses for round-hole punch cards was for toll tickets on east coast turnpikes, to

2030 – When Computers become Human

record where the vehicle entered and to charge the toll upon exit.

2030 – When Computers become Human

As early as 1725, these cards with round holes were used for controlling textile looms. In 1890, Herman Hollerith designed and developed the first punch card machine after contracting with the federal government to process the results of the 1880 census. His design was based upon the Jacquard loom[2], and the working system was completed in just three years.

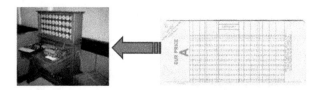

His machine saved the US government $5 million, a good part of the budget in those days. Hollerith later formed a company which today is known as IBM.

---

[2] Jacquard also influenced Charles Babbage, who used punch cards to control the sequence of computations in his analytical engine.

2030 – When Computers become Human

Interestingly, the 60 million cards punched in the 1890 census *(presumably one per person in the United States)* were fed manually into the machine. The counts for each column were displayed in dials on the face of the tabulator.

A "sorter" attached to the machine would be activated by certain hole combination and the result was a set of statistics *(i.e., the number of married men over 50 with fulltime jobs).*

The remarkable growth of IBM in its early years is attributable in great part to the "IBM card", as the punch card came to be known. In IBM's first half-century, the data on punch cards held nearly all the world's collected data.

In my early years at IBM, I wrote programs on a punch-card machine, sorted them on a punch-card sorter whenever I dropped a deck, and fed them into an IBM Model 30 computer, which filled a good-sized room and had the power of today's iPhone. Punch cards were the foundation of early mainframe computers, and for IBM, extremely profitable.

2030 – When Computers become Human

In 1928, IBM transformed and standardized the punch card to be the exact size of a dollar bill, with rectangular holes and 80 columns, some of which *(thank Heaven)* could be used as sequence numbers after very tired programmers on the night shift dropped a deck.

A cottage industry of "service bureaus" was born, with rooms full of punch card machines, sorters and clerks who provided services for data entry and tabulation.

Farnsworth's "Camera Tube"

Now that we had an "engine" that calculates, makes logical decisions, has an input medium *(the punch card)* and an output device *(a printer),* the only thing missing was a display *(a monitor).*

In June of 2014, I was privileged to spend an evening with Phil Savenick at his sprawling home in Westwood, California, next door to UCLA. Phil is a former Disney animation executive, filmmaker, artist, and historian, and has an intense interest in television history.

At the center of Phil's home is a museum dedicated to television history, and a shrine to Philo T. Farnsworth, the pioneer of the technology that made modern television possible.

2030 – When Computers become Human

Philo T. Farnsworth, born in 1906, was raised in a poor home with no electricity. In 1919, his family moved to his Uncle Albert's 240-acre ranch near Rigby, Idaho, to sharecrop. Fortunately, the ranch had not only electricity but also a cache of science magazines like Popular Science in the attic.

Philo's thirst for knowledge opened up a whole world of creativity and inventiveness. One day, while driving a farm vehicle, Philo looked at the newly plowed field, and what he saw was evenly parallel lines, row after row. It occurred to him that an image could be sliced into such rows, back and forth, and then each row could be transmitted in a continuous sequence. Thus the "raster" image was born.

At age 14, he used a lens to direct light into a glass camera tube and invented what was later known as a vacuum tube. In his chemistry class in Rigby, Idaho, Farnsworth sketched out his vacuum tube, as shown below.

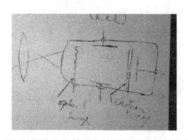

2030 – When Computers become Human

Although neither his teacher nor his fellow students grasped the implications of his concept, he had created the fundamental architecture that would launch and revolutionize the television industry.

In 1926, he scraped together enough funds to continue his scientific work and he moved to San Francisco with his new wife, Elma "Pem" Gardner Farnsworth. The following year, he unveiled his all-electronic television prototype—the first of its kind—made possible by a video camera tube or "image dissector." This was the same device that Farnsworth had sketched in his chemistry class as a teenager.

In 1927, he took a glass slide, smoked it with carbon and scratched a single line on it. This was placed in a carbon arc projector and shone on to the photocathode of his vacuum tube.

Between 1926 and 1929, Farnsworth was consumed by a lengthy legal battle with RCA and other corporate giants. He won the case in court, and his most convincing evidence was the sketch of his vacuum tube.

2030 – When Computers become Human

Philo was ultimately granted Patent #1,773,981 on August 25, 1930, for the cathode ray tube (CRT) and began to receive royalties from RCA and other manufacturers.

In 1930, his wife, "Pem" Farnsworth became the first television actress. In early television filming, she could not face the camera directly because the lights were so hot, and she was required to move away completely after only a few moments.

Pem Gardner Farnsworth, the first TV star!

By the age of 64, Farnsworth held more than 300 United States and foreign patents, most of which formed the foundation of the television industry as it swept the world and changed the nature of modern civilization.

The First Nonmechanical Computer

The earliest calculators were mechanical and controlled by pushbuttons or levers. They were driven by gears, cams, belts or shafts.

 In 1937, J.V. Atanasoff, a professor of physics and mathematics at Iowa State University, built the first non-mechanical computer, called the Atanasoff-Berry (ABC) computer. It was the first automatic digital computer.

By 1941, Atanasoff and his graduate student, Clifford Berry, created the first "multi-tasking" computer that could solve 29 equations simultaneously.

2030 – When Computers become Human

The Atanasoff-Berry computer is sometimes credited with being the first to store information on its main memory. However, this computer was not programmable. It was designed solely to solve linear equations.

There is some debate about whether the "Berry" was really the first digital computer. Some computer historians give this credit to John Mauchly and Presper Eckert, creators of the ENIAC computer, discussed in the next section.

Other noteworthy developments in this area:

In 1937, George Stibitz of Bell Labs constructed a 1-bit binary "adder", which was one of the first binary computers.

In 1940, also at Bell Labs, Stibitz and Samuel Williams built a "Model I Relay Calculator", which could operate on complex numbers.

In 1941, developers at the German Aeronautical Research Institute completed the first operational programmable calculator, which supported floating point numbers.

2030 – When Computers become Human

1n 1943, at team *(that included Turing)* at the Government Code and Cypher School in England completed a machine dedicated to cipher-breaking, the first decryption machine used in World War II.

In 1943, the same team also developed a programmable calculator, where the program as well as data were read in from paper tapes.

Early Mainframes

The earliest computers, called "mainframes", were designed and developed with the architecture shown to the right: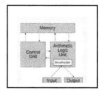

 In 1943-1944, the first electronic computer arrived. It was the Electronic Numerical Integrator and Calculator (ENIAC), financed by the U.S. Army and designed by two University of Pennsylvania professors, John Mauchly and J. Presper Eckert.

The ENIAC is now considered to be the grandfather of digital computers. It filled a 20x40 foot room and had 18,000 vacuum tubes. It was digital and capable of being reprogrammed to solve a broad array of numerical problems.

2030 – When Computers become Human

The ENIAC was initially designed for the Army to calculate artillery firing tables based upon the ballistics of weapons at that time. The media portrayed it as "a Giant Brain", with a breakthrough speed of 1,000 times that of electro-mechanical machines.

Shortly after the end of World War II, the ENIAC was programmed to analyze the feasibility of developing a hydrogen bomb.

 In 1946, Mauchly and Eckert left the University of Pennsylvania and received funding from the Census Bureau to build the UNIVAC, the first commercial computer for business and government data processing.

The increasing demand for large computers was triggered when "second generation" transistors replaced vacuum-tubes in the late 1950s. This spurred development in hardware and software, but early manufacturers commonly built small numbers of each model, targeting narrowly defined vertical markets.

2030 – When Computers become Human

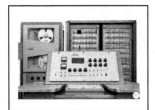 The NEAC 2203 computer was one of the first transistorized computers. It was developed in Japan in 1960 for the purpose of managing Japan's Kinki Nippon Railways online reservation system. It supported both Roman and Japanese character sets and may have been the world's first bilingual computer.

IBM was a pioneer of advancements in the power and capability of mainframes in the forties, fifties and sixties. The first automatic digital calculator in the United States, built for Harvard University in 1944, was named the Automatic Sequence Controlled Calculator.

Other significant computers in the IBM chronology:

1946: the IBM 603 Electronic Multiplier, the first calculator to be placed in production.

1948: the successful IBM 604 Electronic Calculating Punch.

1949: The Card Programmable Calculator (CPC), the first IBM product designed specifically for use in data service centers.

2030 – When Computers become Human

1952: the IBM 701, the company's first commercially available scientific computer.

1953: the IBM 650 Magnetic Drum Calculator, the largest selling computer in the 1950s, and the IBM 702 Electronic Data Processing Machine, with data and programs stored on tape drives.

1954: The Naval Ordnance Research Calculator (NORC), for many years the fastest computer in the World, and the IBM 705 Electronic Data Processing Machine, successor to the 702, with twice its memory.

1956: the SAGE (Semi-Automatic Ground Environment) AN/FSQ-7 series of computers, used for a quarter-century in the U.S. air defense system, and the IBM 305 Random Access Memory Accounting Machine (RAMAC), which employed a magnetic disk memory unit for real-time "in-line data processing".

2030 – When Computers become Human

IBM's "big iron" Data Processing Division (DPD) was formed in 1956 to focus on the design, manufacturing, distribution and marketing of mainframe "super-computers".

Early computers in this category were:

1958: the IBM 7090, the first commercial airline reservation system, employing the proprietary SABRE software.

1961: the IBM 7030 "Stretch" supercomputer, the most powerful computer in the world at that time.

Mainframes eventually gave way to mini-computers and word processing machines that could serve the needs of small businesses.

Programming Languages

 Ada Lovelace, the daughter of Lord Byron Lovelace, was born in 1815 and is considered to be the first programmer. She had a passion for technology and mathematics. Although she married an aristocrat, William Lord King, her true soul mate was Charles Babbage. Babbage is given credit for inventing the Difference Engine *(and later, the Analytical Engine),* but he was exasperated that the logarithm tables within these engines were fraught with errors and could not be relied upon by navigators, astronomers and bankers.

Ada enlightened a frustrated Babbage with her "Ada's Algorithm", which envisioned that the Analytical Engine could be applied to any process that manipulated data. Her translation of data into a process stored within an "engine" was truly the first programming language.

Unfortunately, Ada never received any remuneration for her algorithm, and only used her theory to bet on horses. She ran up huge debts and died relatively unknown at age 36 of uterine cancer.

2030 – When Computers become Human

Ada's algorithmic concept led to the development of early programming "languages", such as Plan Calculus in 1945. The programs were actually "wired" into electromechanical computers and controlled by toggle switches on the computer's panel, as shown above.

As mainframes became more widely used in most industries, the need arose for large and even mid-size enterprises in commerce, the military and government to rely on in-house computer programming departments. Resources for designing and developing programs for general purpose computers were in short supply, and early programming methods were mostly at the "machine" level and employed constructs of ones and zeros (bits) to form computer instructions.

2030 – When Computers become Human

Assembly language, first created for the EDSAC computer in 1949, is a low-level (binary level) programming language that was first input to mainframe computers on punch cards or magnetic tape. Typically, a single program would run on a 1940s-era computer and multi-tasking did not exist.

Programs were written in very low-level instructions and then converted to executable machine instructions by utility programs called Assemblers.

There is typically a one-to-one relationship between an assembly language instruction, written by the programmer, and a machine language instruction, stored in the computer. For example, the "move" instruction is translated to hex 32 (0 – F).

A typical program instruction sequence might load a value from memory into a register (L, or LOAD), compare a register value with a value in memory (C, or COMPARE) and branch to a different part of the program depending upon whether the comparison was true or false (BC, or BRANCH ON CONDITION).

2030 – When Computers become Human

Because of the need to write commercial programs at a much higher level, early programming language developers recognized the need for English-like high-level languages.

Grace Hopper led a team at Remington Rand in 1959 that developed COBOL[3], the first commercial high-level programming language. It was the first user-friendly business-oriented programming language.

Once COBOL programs were entered from data entry devices, they were stored on media and then compiled, and converted into machine language. However, unlike the assembler, a single COBOL instruction would expand to hundreds, if not thousands, of machine instructions in the computer.

------

[33] Common Business-Oriented Language

2030 – When Computers become Human

Examples of COBOL instructions:

MOVE 'Pete' TO EMPLOYEE-NAME

COMPUTE SALARY = MONTHLY * 12

PERFORM 2500-PROCESS-EMPLOYEES

    UNTIL END-OF-FILE[4]

IF MONTHLY-SALARY > 4000

  PERFORM 3000-SALARIED-EMPLOYEES

      ELSE

        PERFORM 3100-HOURLY

      END-IF

---

[4] COBOL programs could contain Procedures which could be executed iteratively.

2030 – When Computers become Human

Almost immediately, COBOL standards were established by the American National Standards Institute (ANSI) so that input to compilers on any mainframe computer would be standardized, but the output of the compiler depended upon its manufacturer and design. COBOL was designed for the development of business applications, and typical processed files on tape drives, or on large portable disk drives. Later, as database systems such as IMS or DB2 were developed, COBOL was enhanced to process hierarchical or relational databases.

A fault in the language not realized until the 90s was that many COBOL programs were written to store the year as a two-digit number.

As a result, most large companies scrambled during the 1990s to hire "Y2K" teams to convert all programs and data to 4-digit years[5]. The teams were so capable that the predicted doomsday on 1/1/2000 never occurred. Not many Y2K team members celebrated New Year's Eve 1999 completely calm or sober.

---

[5] I worked on a Y2K team at Chevron in late 1999.

2030 – When Computers become Human

In the mid-50s, it was recognized that mathematicians and scientists required a more algebraic and formula-oriented programming language. FORTRAN (**FOR**mula **TRAN**slator) was born.

In the late 1940s and early 1950s, John Backus at IBM assembled and guided a team of young men and women with a specific goal: to develop a programming language that could solve mathematical problems. His team consisted of a cryptographer, a chess wizard, programmers, mathematicians and engineers.

FORTRAN was designed for iterative processes, or "Loops", that continued until an intended result was achieved[6].

In 1975, Backus was awarded the National Medal of Science, and two years later, the prestigious Turing Award.

---

[6] Problem was that if the intended result were never achieved, the program would go into an "infinite loop".

2030 – When Computers become Human

Examples of FORTRAN statements:

```
SUBROUTINE SUB1(X, DUMSUB)

INTEGER N, X

EXTERNAL DUMSUB

COMMON /GLOBALS/ N

IF(X .LT. N)THEN

X = X + 1

PRINT *, 'x = ', X

CALL DUMSUB (X, DUMSUB)

END IF

END
```

In 1965, The **PL/1** programming language was released by IBM. PL/1 was developed by IBM at its Hursley, England development lab. Before its commercial release to the general public, PL/1 was employed for internal manufacturing applications at IBM. *I was fortunate enough to head up one of the first PL/1 projects at IBM, which managed an assembly line process, and I worked closely with the development team in*

2030 – When Computers become Human

Hursley to resolve early bugs in the language. Later, I taught PL/1 at IBM.

PL/1 brought to programmers a mix of COBOL's business-program capabilities and FORTRAN's mathematical and scientific functions. Like COBOL, it is procedural and English-like. Like FORTRAN, it is used for numerical computation, scientific computing and even systems programming.

One of PL/1's strengths is bit and character string manipulation, which don't exist in COBOL and FORTRAN. It has many powerful Built-in Functions which can be invoked from within the main program, reducing coding time considerably.

Examples of PL/1 statements:

```
DCL           ALPHABET CHAR(26) INIT('ABC');
DCL    BIN_NUMBER FIXED    BIN(31) INIT(99);
DCL PIC_NUMBER PIC'99V.99' INIT(99.9);

IF              (GTO_DELTA=5)              &
(RETURN_TO_DEPART='N')

THEN   PUT   LIST   ('RETURN=   '||ORIG_DTE||'
'||ORIG_TIM||'                '||APPL_KVL);
IF            THIS_IS_TRUE        =        YES
```

2030 – When Computers become Human

```
THEN          CALL          YOU_ARE_RIGHT;
ELSE CALL YOU_ARE_WRONG;
```

Web Programming Languages

Most businesses today require a web page (or a set of web pages) to market their products and services and, in most cases, take orders. Business executives are typically not tech-savvy and require the services of a web designer and developer. Many implementations of a website are linked to eCommerce sites for the purpose of receiving and fulfilling orders, and to search engines like Google to market their services and products and bring their site to the top of the first page of search results.

The most common website development languages and their specific use by developers are:

HTML

HTML (Hypertext Markup Language) is the language of choice for developing the layout and structure of a website. It creates the look and feel or the site, the means of navigating from page to page, and the "keywords" that will take searchers to the site. HTML is dynamic and is the vehicle for creating a beautiful web site with minimal code.

CSS

CSS (Cascading Style Sheets) is the language that developers use to "style" a website. It is used to describe how a website is presented to a user. It adds or modifies colors, backgrounds, layouts and fonts to the site.

There are three different types of CSS Styles:

- ❖ Internal – this type allows styling of a single web page. In HTML, the following code may be added to the heading: <style type="text/css">.
- ❖ External – this style type is much more efficient than Internal, since you can add a single external .css file, which styles all pages in the entire website.
- ❖ Inline – this CSS type is used to style a specific element on a web page and is rarely used.

JAVA

JAVA is one of the most popular website development languages. It is used for the development of content for games, apps and software particularly in Android apps. Currently, over 15 billion devices are using JAVA.

JAVASCRIPT

JAVASCRIPT is used by game and app developers to add interactive elements to websites.

PYTHON

PYTHON is one of the easiest website development languages to use. Amateurs may host their own "do-it-yourself" websites employ PYTHON because it is easy to learn, has simple syntax and a library of built-in modules.

.NET

.NET (pronounced dot net) is a framework that is used to develop mobile or Windows-based apps. Like PYTHON, it has a huge collection of predefined class libraries which support complex data structures.

The Chip Emerges

From the UNIVAC to the desktop PC, computers continue to process faster and become remarkably smaller. A major contributor to this transition was the replacement of the vacuum tube with the transistor.

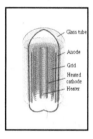

The type of vacuum tube used in early computers was a triode, invented by Lee de Forest in 1906. It was comprised of a cathode and a plate, separated by a control grid, and suspended in a glass vacuum tube, as shown ---→

The control grid controls the flow of electrons in either direction. By making it negative, electrons are repelled back to the cathode. When positive, electrons are attracted to the plate. It was an effective on-off switch or "gate", but it consumed excessive power and gave off tremendous heat. In addition, these tubes failed often in large computers and were unreliable.

2030 – When Computers become Human

Contrast vacuum tubes with transistors, which were a game-changing contribution to the evolution of the computer as we know it  today. Invented in 1947 at Bell Laboratories by engineers John Bardeen and Walter Brattain, it was a reliable solid-state electronic switch, considerably smaller than the tube, and it gave off little heat.

 In 1948, Bell associate William Shockley invented the bipolar junction transistor (BJT), which relied on two types of semiconductors for its operation. BJTs can be used as amplifiers, switches or oscillators (for timing).

 Later on, many BJTs were combined in large numbers on the first integrated circuits, invented in 1958 by Jack Kilby and Robert Noyce. Integrated circuits later came to be known as computer chips, called "chips" because they are built on a slice of silicon.

Other Developments

2030 – When Computers become Human

1964: Douglas Engelbart demonstrated a prototype of the modern computer, with a mouse and a simple graphical user interface (GUI). This marked the transition of the computer from a specialized machine for scientists and mathematicians, to technology that is more accessible and user-friendly for the general public.

1970: The newly formed Intel unveils the Intel 1103, the first Dynamic Access Memory (DRAM) chip.

2014: IBM develops the True North neural chip, which simulates functions of neurons, synapses, and other brain activity. It uses  no more power than a hearing aid and mimics the way human brains recognize patterns. It is used globally for facial recognition and in the sensors on autonomous devices.

Moore's Law

Moore's law is the observation in 1965 by Gordon Moore, co-founder of Intel, that the number of transistors per square inch on integrated circuits had doubled every year  since the integrated circuit was invented, while maintaining the same price point. His prediction has proven to be quite accurate for almost 50 years[7].

Moore's law turned out to be quite accurate, even today: the law is still a guide in the semi-conductor industry for long-term planning and establishing targets and goals for research and development.

---

[7] In 2019, Nvidia CEO Jensen Huang declared that **Moore's Law** is dead and from now on it will be more costly and technically difficult to double the number of transistors driving processing power.

2030 – When Computers become Human

The capabilities of many digital electronic devices correlated with Moore's law:

> ➢ Microprocessor prices
>
> ➢ Memory capacity
>
> ➢ Robotic sensors
>
> ➢ The number and size of pixels in digital cameras

Early Personal Computers

1974-1977: **Personal computers** hit the market, including the Altair, IBM 5100, RadioShack's TRS-80, and the Commodore PET.

1975: The **IBM 5100** becomes the first commercially available "portable" computer.

1976: **Steve Jobs** and **Steve Wozniak** start Apple Computers in a garage and roll out the **Apple I**.

1977: Radio Shack's initial production run of the **TRS-80** was just 3,000. It sold like crazy.

1981: The first IBM personal computer, code named "**Acorn**", is introduced. It uses Microsoft's MS-DOS operating system. It has an Intel chip, two floppy disks and an optional color monitor.

1983: **Apple's Lisa** is the first personal computer with a GUI[8]. It also featured a drop-down menu and icons.

---

[8] Graphic User Interface

PART II. TRANSFORMATION

THE TURING TEST

When will a computer's intelligence equal human intelligence? In 1951, the British mathematician Alan Turing proposed that, if a person of either gender were in one room, and a computer were in another room, if a "judge" could not determine from which room the response to his questions came, artificial intelligence could not be distinguished from human intelligence.

The movie about Turing's test, called **The Imitation Game** was released in 2014. The movie portrays the life of Turing, starring Benedict Cumberbatch as Turing, and Keira Knightley as Joan Clark, his star crypto analyst.

Artificial Intelligence

Artificial intelligence ("AI") is a concept where a machine perceives its environment through sensors and makes decisions or takes actions that maximizes the possibility of a successful result. This concept was introduced commercially in 1990 at the Massachusetts Institute of Technology (MIT) and found its way into homes as the Roomba vacuum cleaner.

Early research into artificial intelligence was highly technical and specialized, focusing on accomplishing a specific outcome. The evolution from a primitive robot to the self-driving car demonstrates how far we have come. The areas of current AI research continue to focus on reasoning, development of a knowledge base, design and planning, learning, natural language processing *(communication)*, perception, and the ability to manipulate objects. This field is based upon the goal that intelligence can be so precisely emulated in a machine that the machine will simulate a human. This raises the ethical concern of creating artificial beings endowed with human-like intelligence.

2030 – When Computers become Human

Greek mythology perceived of "thinking machines" such as the bronze robot of Hephaestus, and Pygmalion's Galatea. Every major civilization believed in human likenesses with intelligence. By the 20th century, artificial beings were introduced in fiction, as in Shelley's Frankenstein.

In the summer of 1956, academic research in AI was founded at a conference at Dartmouth College. Three attendees became the leaders of AI research for several decades. Their research produced astonishing results *(at the time)* such as computers with the ability to speak English. By the mid-sixties, research in the United States was heavily funded by the Department of Defense and laboratories or think tanks emerged throughout the world.

Artificial intelligence is now used for medical diagnosis and even for surgery *(i.e., Intuitive Surgical's da Vinci robotic surgery system)*.

2030 – When Computers become Human

Although research into AI in the late fifties focused on imitating human intelligence, linguist, philosopher and logician Noam Chomsky[9] and others at MIT explored cognitive science, a field aimed at understanding the mental form and rules that are the foundation of perceptual and cognitive abilities. Chomsky's work has influenced research not only into AI, but also in the fields of cognitive science, music theory, political science, and programming language theory.

In 1979, exploration of artificial intelligence emerged in the form of a nonprofit society called the Association for the Advancement of Artificial Intelligence (AAAI).

This society focused on advancing the understanding of the mechanisms that underlie thought and intelligent behavior, and how this behavior can be embodied in machines. Like most AI societies, they are partially funded by

[9] Born December 7, 1928

[10] His license plate frame read "Do the arithmetic or be doomed to talk nonsense".

member dues and they seek donations and grants.

The term Artificial Intelligence is believed to have been coined in 1956 by John McCarthy[10] when he assembled the first academic conference on the subject at Stanford. He focused on applied mathematical logic in computer programs to support the concept of AI. He was part of development teams that built early programming languages such as LISP and ALGOL. In 1960, LISP became the programming language of choice for AI applications.

No one has ever disputed the computer's ability to process logic and arrive at a result. But most people will question whether a machine can *think*. Of course, Bill Clinton might say "It depends upon what the meaning of *think* is".

Significant advances have been made in AI over the past 65 years, particularly with search and machine learning algorithms, and with the mass integration of statistical analysis with the ultimate goal of understanding the world at large.

2030 – When Computers become Human

AI expectations always seemed to outpace reality in the 80s and 90s. Significant breakthroughs have been promised *"in ten years"* for the past sixty years. After decades of research, no computer has come close to passing the Turing test, although IBM's Watson is getting better and better at playing chess. Further research is encouraged by the Leobner Prize established in 1995 and the associated Turing Test Competition, with a $100,000 reward for development of a system indistinguishable from a human.

In an effort to build a computer that could win a game of chess against a *master*, two approaches evolved: Type-A programs, which would use pure brute force, examine thousands of moves, and use a min-max search algorithm to specify the next move. Or Type-B programs which would use specialized heuristics and 'strategic' AI, examining only a few, key candidate moves.

The Type-A approach was successful in May 1997, when an IBM computer called Deep Blue® beat world chess champion Garry Kasparov after a six-game match: two wins for IBM, one for the champion and three draws.

2030 – When Computers become Human

By 2014, Type-A brute force programs were chosen over Type-B due to the exponentially increasing processing power of computer chips, and to vast data storage available in the cloud.

The next frontier for Type-A programs will be to win at the ancient Asian game of **Go**. Whereas chess has a branching factor *(all possible moves)* of 40, Go's approaches 200.

Expert systems, a subset of AI, attempt to model human expertise in one or more *specific* knowledge areas. These systems have three basic components:

> ➢ A cumulative knowledge base.

> ➢ An inference engine to process input.

> ➢ An input/output (I/O) interface to interact with the user.

2030 – When Computers become Human

Expert systems are characterized by:

> - The use of symbolic logic rather than numeric calculations

> - Data-driven processing

> - A knowledge base for a specific area of exploration

> - Interpretation of its results in a way that is understandable and useful by the user.

The dreams of scientists and science fiction go far beyond artificial intelligence and currently we are witnessing remarkable breakthroughs, which will be presented in the following chapters. The ultimate goal seems to be autonomous *(see page 110)* "thinking" systems that are free of human guidance or interference.

We will ultimately arrive at a point when devices provide spontaneous and unsolicited advice, knowledge and guidance to their "masters".

Ray Kurzweil in his book **The Singularity is Near** (see page 93) predicted that when computer processing is equivalent to the speed of the human brain, we will have computers as intelligent as humans.

Machine Learning

Machine Learning (ML) differs from Artificial Intelligence (AI), discussed in the previous chapter, in that AI is a broader endeavor to create intelligent machines that can simulate human thinking and behavior. Machine Learning is an application of AI that allows machines to learn from aggregated data and input from sensors without the learning process being explicitly programmed.

Until the 1950s, computers contained programs which performed complex calculations, manipulated data, and navigated within them by making logical decisions based upon a condition being true or false.

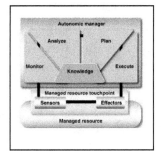

Machine learning, on the other hand, enables a computer to make decisions based upon analysis of historical data and human decisions without being explicitly programmed. The result is an ever-changing accumulation of structured data so that the machine *(i.e., computer)* can predict future human actions and decisions based upon accumulated learning.

Machine Learning expands and improves by analyzing data within a collection of datasets that are related to one another. These datasets can be **Numerical** *(i.e., salaries, temperature, stock prices, etc.)*, **Categorical** *(i.e., Yes/No, True/False, Day/Night, etc.)*, or **Ordinal** *(i.e., measured on the relationship of one data point to another)*.

Robotics

Is a mechanical bird a robot? Back in 350 B.C., Greek mathematician Archytas built a steam-powered "Pigeon" that was history's earliest study of flight, and probably the first model airplane.

Along came Greek philosopher Aristotle 28 years later who wrote:

"If every tool, when ordered, or even of its own accord, could do the work that befits it... then there would be no need either of apprentices for the master workers or of slaves for the lords."

...suggesting how nice it would be to have a few robots around, while envisioning singularity.

Move forward to 1495, when Leonardo Da Vinci built a mechanical device that looked like an armored knight. The mechanisms inside, mostly gears and pulleys, were designed to amuse royalty and move as though there were a real person inside.

By 1770, Swiss clock makers led by the inventor of the modern wristwatch Pierre Jaquet-Droz created three dolls to entertain royalty, one that could write, another that played music, and a third that drew pictures.

2030 – When Computers become Human

In 1898, Nikola Tesla *(does that name ring a bell?)* built and demonstrated a remote-controlled robotic boat at Madison Square Garden. Did he ever dream that a successor robot with his name would be powered by batteries?

Now let's look at the evolution toward the modern-day robot with built-in artificial intelligence. The person credited with introducing the word "Robot" in 1921 was Czech writer Karel Capek in his play **R.U.R.** *(Rossum's Universal Robots)*. The Czech word "robota" means "compulsory labor".

Beginning in 1940, Issac Asimov wrote a series of short stories about robots. The first was **A Strange Playfellow** (later renamed "Robbie"). In 1950, all of his short stories were compiled into a single volume: **I, Robot**.

2030 – When Computers become Human

Azimov's most important contribution to the field of robotics was his **Three Laws of Robotics**:

1. A robot may not injure a human being, or, through inaction, allow a human being to come to harm.

2. A robot must obey the orders given it by human beings except where such orders would conflict with the First Law.

3. A robot must protect its own existence as long as such protection does not conflict with the First or Second Law.

The employment of the third law, while ignoring laws 1 and 2, is demonstrated by *Hal* in "**2001-A Space Odyssey**".

In the 20th century, and even more rapidly in the 21st century, robotic technology has advanced rapidly. Now robots can assemble other machines, and some robots are mistaken for human beings.

The robot in the mid-20th century was a curiosity, even appearing on the Tonight Show in 1966. Then robots found a place in industrial manufacturing and spread rapidly to Japan, South Korea and throughout Europe. In the mid-sixties, the first operational industrial robot in North America worked in a candy factory in

2030 – When Computers become Human

Kitchener, Ontario. It didn't even have to be fed, and it worked well below minimum wage.

Robots have found a place in other vertical markets, such as toys and entertainment, military weapons and search and rescue. Some even became "self-repairing" such as W. Grey Walter's Elmer and Elsie *(aka "turtle robots")*, which found their charging station when their batteries were low *(1948).*

 A major milestone in force feedback *(haptic technology)* was Raymond Goertz's first tele-operated articulated arm *(1951).*

George Devol and Joseph Engelberger, in 1954, are credited with designing the first *truly* programmable robot. Named UNIMATE, it became the launch product for their company, Unimation, believed to be the first company to manufacture and market robots. The company is still in production today.

2030 – When Computers become Human

In 1957, the Soviet Union surpassed the United States by creating Sputnik I, the world's first autonomous artificial satellite.

Research laboratories dedicated to producing robots with human-like artificial intelligence sprung up in universities. Among the first were teams at MIT, Stanford Research Institute (SRI), Stanford University and the University of Edinburgh.

Carnegie Mellon established the Robotics Institute in 1979, dedicated to integrating robotic technologies into everyday activities. They are a leader in innovative research in diverse robotics-related fields, and sponsor many academic programs from grade-school summer camps to PhD curricula.

In the late sixties, *walking* robots *(some with arms)* hit the scene. Breakthroughs included:

> ➢ A remote-controlled walking "truck" by R. Mosher

> ➢ SRI's "Shakey", a mobile robot equipped with a vision system and controlled by a room-size computer.

2030 – When Computers become Human

- ➢ The Stanford Arm, which was the first successful computer controlled robotic arm.

- ➢ WAP-1, the first biped robot with artificial muscles, that could turn while walking and climbing up and down stairs.

- ➢ The Russian Academy of Science's first six-legged walking vehicle. Why six legs? It was developed as a prototype for walking on rough terrain such as the Moon and controlled by algorithms that responded to sensors such as degree of climb or descent, or relative position of each of its six legs.

2030 – When Computers become Human

The 70's and early 80's generation of robots focused on robots that simulated the limbs of a human being. Included in this generation are:

(**1973**) The WABOT I, a full-scale anthropomorphic robot, with a processor that controlled limbs, vision and conversation. It was thought to have the mental ability of an 18-month-old and these kids know what they want!

(**1973**) Cincinnati Milacron's T3, the first commercial minicomputer-controlled industrial robot, used primarily for welding. It didn't even wear goggles!

(**1975**) Victor Schenman at Unimation developed the Programmable Universal Manipulation Arm *(PUMA),* used in many industrial operations. It's advanced design, flexibility and precision results in high quality industrial products with few defects.

(**1980**) The WL-9DR "quasi-dynamic" walking robot, controlled by a microcomputer, takes one step every 10 seconds. It was designed for "plane walking", which includes straight walking, sideway walking and turning. The designer's goal was for the robot's movements to be as smooth and rapid as man's walking.

(**1981**) The Titan II and III, a quadruped which can climb stairs.

(**1990**) iRobot Corporation produces domestic and military robots, dedicated to making a difference in people's lives. Its most well- known products in the nineties are the Roomba *(vacuum cleaning)*, the Scooba *(floor scrubbing)* and the Brava *(floor mopping)*.

2030 – When Computers become Human

ROBOTS IN THE 21ST CENTURY

In the 21st century, robotics products emerged to support business efficiency as well as the replacement of workers with mundane jobs. A leader in R&D for these commercial products is iRobot Corporation, moving from vacuum cleaners to video collaboration and the world of "bots".

Their 21st century products include:

Ava 500, the Video Collaboration Robot. Its monitor on a pedestal allows business associates to establish a physical presence from a remote location with complete freedom of movement.

The **RP-VITA® Remote Presence Robot**. It gives the medical community remote presence for patient care that combines autonomous navigation and mobility from the **iRobot** with telemedicine technology from **InTouch** Health.

The **iRobot Ava Mobile Robotics Platform**, a solution suitable for 3rd party development and a wide range of applications. It is capable of autonomous navigation in our complex real world.

2030 – When Computers become Human

In 2014, Loew's introduced robotic shopping assistants, the first retail robot of its kind in the US. The OSHbot greets customers, asks them if they need assistance, and guides them to products of interest. It uses natural language technology, and features two rectangular screens, one for videoconferencing between the shopper and a store's expert, and the others to assist the shopper in locating products. The robot's multi-lingual head features a 3-D scanner for pricing and identifying store specials.

Another area of research in this century is the application of robotics to recognition *(see page 88).* In 2000, Sony announced the Sony Dream Robot (SDR). This robot was able to recognize 10 different facial expressions, express emotion through speech and body language, and walk on rough terrain.

After the World Trade Center attack, iRobot Packbots were employed to search through the rubble for humans, living or dead, and for the recovery of personal items.

2030 – When Computers become Human

The first robotics competition, **Sport for the Mind**, aimed at 9th to 12th graders, combined the excitement of sport with the rigors of science and technology. Under strict rules, limited resources, and time limits, teams of 25 students or more are challenged to raise funds, design a team "brand," hone teamwork skills, and build and program their robots to perform prescribed tasks against a field of competitors. Winners qualified for over $19 million in college scholarships.

Facial recognition has launched many useful applications. It perhaps was first employed for commercial use at many airports throughout the world for the primary purpose of curbing illegal immigration.

Research into facial recognition began in the mid-sixties and was used for mapping features in photographs and comparing the "map" to other photographs. These biometrics are now widely used in security systems and are stored in recognition databases along with fingerprint or eye iris metrics. Combining facial, fingerprint and eye iris biometrics to identify a single unique person is powerful! The technology is widely used in China.

2030 – When Computers become Human

Eventually, robots moved into space. A **robotic spacecraft** has no humans aboard and is usually under *telerobotic*[11] control.

In 2001, MD Robotics of Canada launched the Space Station Remote Manipulator System which was used to assemble the International Space Station.

A *telemanipulator* is a device that is controlled remotely by a human operator. However, if a device has the ability to perform some autonomous work and some work controlled by a human, it is called a **telerobot**. If a device is completely autonomous, it is called a **robot**.

---

[11] Telerobotics is an area of semi-autonomous robotics where spacecraft are controlled either wirelessly or tethered.

2030 – When Computers become Human

Examples of autonomous or semi-autonomous robots are:

> Honda's Advanced Step in Innovative Mobility (ASIMO).

> TOSY's Ping Pong Playing Robot (TOPIO).

> Industrial robots, also called swarm robots.

> Microscopic nanorobots, sometimes imbedded in animals or humans.

> Bio-inspired Robots, inspired by nature.

Today's robots typically have the capability to move around in their environment and are not bound to a physical location. However, industrial robots are usually fixed to an assembly position and have a jointed arm and an end effector *(such as a gripper)*.

This chapter would not be complete without mentioning laparoscopic robot surgery machines. The forerunner in this field is the Da Vinci Surgical System, produced by Intuitive Surgical.

2030 – When Computers become Human

The future of robotics is boundless. Google has developed tiny magnetic particles that can patrol the human body for signs of cancer and other diseases. These nanoparticles, one-thousandth the width of red blood cells, will seek out and attach themselves to cell or proteins inside the body and will be monitored by a magnetic wireless receiver. These magnetic "nanobots" will also carry drugs into the brain.

The Robat is a robotic wing that helps biologists uncover the secret of bat flight. Childlike humanoid robots are now starting to comprehend spoken language. Ping Pong ball-sized robots will swarm together to collectively form a smart liquid.

Polaris is a solar-powered ice-drilling lunar Prospector-Bot. Georgia Tech's 'MacGyver' robots improvise based upon their environment and have been used in search and rescue. Robot sea turtles will carry cargo in their shells.

Drones

Drones are unmanned aerial vehicles with no onboard crew. They can be remotely piloted or autonomous[12]. They are powered by jets, reciprocating engines, electric engines and, more recently, solar powered.

When employed for military use, drones differ from cruise missiles in that drones are recovered after a mission, while cruise missiles impact their targets and are destroyed. A drone may carry and fire munitions, while a cruise missile *is* a munition.

The first recorded use of drones was in 1849 when Austrians attacked Venice, Italy using unmanned balloons loaded with explosives.

Drones that are used in warfare are employed primarily so that human pilots need not risk their lives in missions.

---

[12] The definition of "autonomous" is an entity or device that is self-controlling and not governed by outside forces.

2030 – When Computers become Human

During World War I, the U.S. Navy hired Elmer Sperry, the inventor of the gyroscope, to design and produce unmanned biplanes that could be launched by a catapult, fly over enemy positions and drop "air torpedoes" on the enemy.

The Navy experimented with radio-controlled aircraft that were remotely controlled from another aircraft. These N2C-2 drones were placed in service in 1938.

In 1941, "Project Fox" launched an assault drone with an RCA TV camera in the drone and a TV Screen in the control aircraft. This assault drone successfully torpedoed a German destroyer from 20 miles away.

In World War II, the Navy launched a program called Operation Anvil. These refitted B-24 bombers were filled with explosives and guided by remote control to crash on selected German targets. The remote controls were crude radio-controlled devices linked to motors in the plane's cockpit.

Unfortunately, Operation Anvil was a disaster, mainly because human pilots were required for take-off, guided the plane to a cruising altitude, and then parachute to safety in England.

2030 – When Computers become Human

Many planes crashed before the pilot escaped. The most famous victim was John F. Kennedy's older brother Joseph, one of the program's first pilots. It's ironic that the target of Joseph Kennedy's mission was a Nazi site where scientists were thought to be working on technology that would support the remote delivery of explosives.

With advances in precise rocketry, the development of drones stagnated through the fifties. Advances in cruise missiles were more guidable and could take off and maintain altitude with their stubby little wings.

By the late fifties, the success of targeted drones led to their use in other missions, such as reconnaissance. These drones were used to spy on North Vietnam, Communist China and North Korea in the sixties and seventies.

By the end of the fifties, the only U.S. spy plane active was the U-2. It was a single-engine high altitude aircraft operated by the Air Force. However, they were not drones, but instead were flown by highly trained pilots. In 1960, Gary Powers was shot down over the Soviet Union by a surface to air missile.

2030 – When Computers become Human

Unmanned aerial vehicles were used extensively in the eighties. Their reputation improved dramatically after the Israeli Air Force's victory over the Syrian Air Force in 1982. Israel destroyed dozens of Syrian aircraft with few losses. These drones were used as decoys and electronic signal jammers.

After 9/11, the CIA encouraged the use of armed drones for military operations rather than for surveillance. This led to ethical and management controversy over who could "pull the trigger" and in which situations attacks were permitted.

DRONES FOR THE MASSES

Between 2011 and 2014, China's SZ DJI Technology Company emerged as the world's largest *(by revenue)* consumer drone manufacturer. It currently sells thousands of its 2.8-pound, square footprint devices for about $1000 each.

Almost anyone can pilot DJI's Phantom. With four helicopter-like propellers, it can hover, climb, descend and view terrain below with its high-definition camera. To target a higher-end professional market, DJI developed its next drone, the Inspire.

Search and Rescue teams, particularly with the U.S. Coast Guard, have used the Phantom to search for survivors after natural disasters. The militant group ISIS has used this drone for surveillance in Syria.

2030 – When Computers become Human

Phantoms are the top choice of entrepreneurs. Producers use them for filmmaking, construction and farming. Initially, their use was mostly in defiance of the Federal Aviation Administration's moratorium on commercial drones, primarily because it was difficult to regulate and enforce.

Currently, to fly a **drone** for commercial purposes in the **U.S.** you must obtain a Remote Pilot Certificate from the FAA and pass an Aeronautical Knowledge Test—also known as the Part 107 test—at an FAA-approved knowledge testing center. In addition, you must undergo Transportation Safety Administration (TSA) security screening.

Today, under the US Drone Laws, you may fly personal drones below 400 feet in uncontrolled airspace without specific authorization, but a license is required. Also, you must comply with all restrictions and prohibitions when flying in any airspace, whether controlled or uncontrolled.

2030 – When Computers become Human

DRONES AS PROJECTORS

Tom Frey, Google's esteemed futurist, suggests that in the near future, a video projector mounted in a flying drone could be used to produce special effects at outdoor concerts, or in large stadiums. The projectors could roam around producing spot advertisement, or even subliminal advertising. They could be used for search and rescue to guide lost souls out of a forest, by projecting arrows on the ground. Flying drones could even mask images of humans, to disguise them or prevent them from being monitored.

Speech Recognition – Audrey to Siri

The development of speech recognition technology over the years is comparable to watching a baby's progress from baby-talk to speaking in syllables like "Mama" and "Dada", to building a large spontaneous vocabulary, and then sprinkling words with wit, humor, and inspiration.

Early speech recognition devices at first recognized only numbers. Then, in 1952, Bell Labs developed the Audrey system, which recognized digits spoken by a single voice, after significant "training" by the user.

Ten years later, IBM demonstrated its "Shoebox", a machine that could understand sixteen words spoken in English by some persons, but not by others with accents or unusual pitch.

Research labs sprung up in the late sixties in England, Japan, the Soviet Union, and the United States. Scientists in these labs invented hardware capable of responding to words that contained four vowels and nine consonants.

SPEECH RECOGNITION TAKES OFF

Not surprisingly, the U.S. Department of Defense spurred significant growth in speech recognition, through its DARPA[13] Speech Understanding Research (SUR) program. Out of this program evolved Carnegie-Mellon's "Harpy" speech "understanding" program, which could understand over 1000 words, equivalent to the vocabulary of a 3-year-old.

What is most interesting about speech recognition research at that time is that scientists began to realize that the theory of speech recognition is very closely related to advances in search methodology. This led to the evolution of Siri's voice recognition and response system moving in step with Google's search engine methodology. Of course, Siri is "purer" *(in 2014)* because her responses are unbiased, while Google's search engine results are "ranked" based upon advertising dollars, and somewhat controlled by the effectiveness of search engine optimization.

---

[13] Defense Advanced Research Projects Agency

2030 – When Computers become Human

In the eighties, speech recognition advances focused on predicting intelligent responses. Faster processing speeds resulted in recognizable vocabulary of several thousand words. Today, it has the potential to recognize an almost unlimited number of words in many languages and can even translate from one language to another.

In 1982, Ray Kurzweil's company, Applied Intelligence and Dragon Systems, released speech recognition applications. By 1985, this software had a vocabulary of 1,000 words. Two years later, in 1987, its lexicon reached 20,000 words, entering the realm of human vocabularies, which range from 10,000 to 150,000 words. But accuracy was only 10% in 1993. Two years later, the error rate crossed below 50%.

Dragon Systems released "Naturally Speaking" in 1997, which recognized normal human speech. Progress accelerated primarily due to improved computer performance and larger source text databases. Recently, Kurzweil has collaborated with Google to produce remarkable advances in speech and image recognition.

2030 – When Computers become Human

The "Hidden Markov model", developed by L.E. Baum and his coworkers, applies mathematical algorithms to model language. These statistical models produce a sequence of symbols and quantities that translate sounds to uniform 10-millisecond signals. These models can be trained automatically and improve with usage.

These algorithms use context dependency to respond based upon the environment in which the signals are produced. And, as witnessed with Siri and GPS guidance, the voice can be associated with a single responder, male or female.

The future of Speech Recognition

Speech recognition software technology has made incredible advances in recent years, particularly when imbedded in cell phones. Witness the explosion of people using Apple's Siri, or Samsung's counterpart S Voice.

Speech recognition Bluetooth software in automobiles has improved dramatically. High-end cars like Mercedes and BMW are delivered with separate voice command Help assists and, in the Mercedes the driver is encouraged to use voice commands rather than push buttons. Coupled with integrated phone calling and phone books, speech recognition has made driving safer and reduced accidents caused by distractions such as texting while driving.

Speech recognition and triggered announcements prompted by events in one's calendar, or simply a person's location, is now embedded as a "personal assistant" that assists active people in their day-to-day activities. You can even use voice recognition in apps that control your thermostat, view rooms in your home, turn off lights, close garage doors, and remotely program your DVR.

2030 – When Computers become Human

In the future, expect voice recognition systems to become more conversational and to "remember" your questions and conversations in the past. You won't need to call a specific restaurant to make a reservation. Instead, you'll tell Siri to "make a reservation for Monica and me this evening at our favorite Afghan restaurant at the usual time".

Nuance Communications Dragon Software, the mind of Siri, is now used heavily in business to reduce interaction of callers with human employees. It is commonplace in call centers, where callers must navigate through a series of menus and, in many cases, never speak to a human either because they have gotten the response that they were seeking, or because they hang up in frustration.

Ray Kurzweil: Singularity

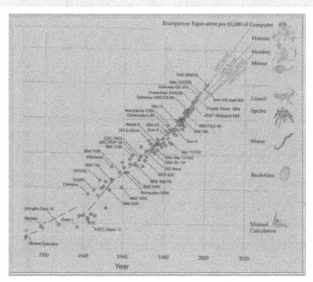

In 2005, inventor and futurist Ray Kurzweil wrote a non-fiction book about artificial intelligence and the future of humanity. His book, **The Singularity Is Near: When Humans Transcend Biology** inspired me to write this book.

Some of the concepts, breakthroughs and predictions in this book are also derived from Kurzweil's previous books, **The Age of Spiritual Machines** (1999), and **The Age of Intelligent Machines** (1990).

2030 – When Computers become Human

His hypothesis is that with accelerating increases in the performance and capacity of computers, along with vast repositories for data "in the clouds", the world will witness a technological singularity, where machine intelligence will be as powerful as human intelligence. He originally predicted that this singularity would occur in 2045, but more recently predicted that it will occur on or before 2030.

As this singularity approaches, the God-given human body will be augmented by genetic alterations, nanotechnology, and artificial intelligence imbedded within the body. This is characterized by Kurzweil as an epoch in where "The Merger of Human Technology with Human Intelligence" occurs.

This countdown to technological singularity can be portrayed graphically as the relationship of a particular computer's power[14] to brains of various animals, and ultimately the human, over time.

---

[14] Power as measured in the number of MIPS available for $1,000, closely adhering to Moore's Law.

2030 – When Computers become Human

This achievement is possible because of the converging advances in genetics, nanotechnology, robotics and artificial intelligence. Kurzweil feels that eventually technology will make it possible to maintain the body *indefinitely*, reverse aging and cure cancer, heart disease and deathly diseases such as Ebola and COVID.

In 2012, Kurzweil published **How to Create a Mind**. In it, he describes the brain and correlates the mind to the computer. His book attempts to convince the reader that it is within our reach to create non-biological intelligence that will soar past our own. Of particular interest in this book is the statement that the target for a full brain simulation now moves to 2023. IBM research in 2014 certainly affirms that direction.

2030 – When Computers become Human

WHAT WILL THE DIFFERENCES BE?

The human response will be based in part on emotions, intuition, involuntary action and ability to recall, while...

The computer's "brain" will produce a response based upon its knowledge base, total recall, and logical decision-making algorithms.

Human decisions may be based partly upon a person's ethics or fears of consequences, while...

The computer will make decisions based purely on logic and its knowledge base *(as a result of ongoing machine learning)*.

Humans may consider their rights and responsibilities when they use information available to them, particularly on the internet, while...

The computer has no conscience and will not be swayed by ethics, legal concerns, religious beliefs, or fear.

2030 – When Computers become Human

The computer's knowledge base is expected to contain accurate and timeless information, while...

the information available to a human may be the results of collaborate efforts that have been tainted by conflicting contributions, or contain targeted and subliminal advertising, or was just down-right wrong (or fake) when it was written.

WHAT IF THE COMPUTER IS MORE INTELLIGENT?

Kurzweil predicts a time when all the computers in the world will have an aggregate intelligence that is more powerful than all human intelligence combined. He claims that intelligence will then radiate outward from the planet until it saturates the universe, maybe around 2045.

2030 – When Computers become Human

As far back as 1968, movies have attempted to humanize and "personalize" the computer. Many of the early movies were not based upon technological advances but were instead mostly science fiction. In 1996, Two Stanford professors, Byron Reeves and Clifford Nass, published the results of various psychological studies that suggested that people treat computers, television and media as real people and real places. We even treat computers with female voices differently from computers with male voices.

Let us look at the striking differences between a movie released in 1968, and another released much later in 2013.

2030 – When Computers become Human

"2001: A SPACE ODYSSEY"

In *1968*, *the film* **2001: A Space Odyssey** hit the big screen. Produced and directed by Stanley Kubrick, the movie was partially inspired by Arthur C. Clarke's short story "**The Sentinel**". An early draft of the film's screenplay was written by both Kubrick and Clarke. This scenario was mostly improvised, rather than based upon the traditional development of a script.

The movie was astoundingly prescient, revolutionizing science fiction and the art of cinema-making. It transformed the way we think about film, by introducing revolutionary special effects, a unique narrative style, philosophical undertones, and unusual choices of classical musical score such as The Blue Danube.

Although Kubrick was afraid of flying, he remarkedly insisted upon the Dawn of Man sequence being filmed as all still shots *(i.e., photographs)* by his second unit in Africa. The crew communicated with Kubrick in London by land line until he got all the shots that he wanted. The still shots were used as backdrops for the movie, and ape-man actors *(mimes)* performed live in front of these backdrops.

2030 – When Computers become Human

The story deals with a series of encounters between ape-like humans and tapirs that results in one party being driven off. Next morning, a tall, thin, rectangular black monolith is seen among the rocks. It is soon determined that an alien force moving through our planetary system has dropped the monolith upon the apes' water hole, and war breaks out.

One ape's pitching of a bone toward the monolith strikes another bone; this event marks a turning point in our evolution: humanoids learn to kill and hunt with weapons, and to walk upright.

The spinning bone segues to spaceships above Earth, and the Monolith on the Moon section of the movie begins.

Thematically, the film deals with elements of human evolution, technology, artificial intelligence and extraterrestrial life. **2001-A Space Odyssey** is notable for its scientific accuracy, pioneering special effects, and minimal use of dialogue.

2030 – When Computers become Human

The spaceship Discovery, 80 million miles above earth, is commanded by Dave Bowman and BBC news is reported on Earth. There are five humans aboard, but three astronauts are in hibernation to save air and food; they will be needed at the destination for a survey.

The sixth member of the crew is the **HAL9000** computer, which can talk and mimic the human brain. The BBC newscaster interviews Dave and Frank together and then speaks to Hal, who states that "he" is foolproof and incapable of error.

This is where Hal starts to exhibit human traits, including self-confidence, superiority, and stubbornness. Frank and Hal play chess and, of course, Hal wins.

Dave sketches and shows his artwork to Hal. HAL expresses some concern about the mission and secrecy. Hal then announces there is a problem with the AE-35 unit, and it will fail with 100% certainty within 72 hours.

2030 – When Computers become Human

HAL's confidence and superiority is evidenced by the following excerpts of dialogue from the movie:

HAL: "I am putting myself to the fullest possible use, which is all I think that any conscious entity can ever hope to do".

[Regarding the supposed failure of the parabolic antenna on the ship, which HAL himself falsified]

HAL: "It can only be attributable to human error".

Dave Bowman: "Open the pod bay doors, HAL".

HAL: "I'm sorry, Dave. I'm afraid I can't do that".

Dave Bowman: "What are you talking about, HAL?"

HAL: "This mission is too important for me to allow you to jeopardize it".

Dave Bowman: "I don't know what you're talking about, HAL".

HAL: "I know that you and Frank were planning to disconnect me, and I'm afraid that's something I cannot allow to happen".

2030 – When Computers become Human

Dave Bowman: "HAL, I won't argue with you anymore! Open the doors!"

HAL: "Dave, this conversation can serve no purpose anymore. Goodbye".

[on Dave's return to the ship, after HAL has killed the rest of the crew]

HAL: "Look Dave, I can see you're really upset about this. I honestly think you ought to sit down calmly, take a stress pill, and think things over".

[HAL's shutdown – starting to exhibit fear]

HAL: "I'm afraid. I'm afraid, Dave. Dave, my mind is going. ... My mind is going. There is no question about it. I can feel it. I can feel it. ... I'm afraid".

[HAL gradually slows down and, at the end, sings "Daisy"]

HAL: "Good afternoon, gentlemen. I am a HAL 9000 computer. I became operational at the H.A.L. plant in Urbana, Illinois on the 12th of January 1992. My instructor was Mr. Langley, and he taught me to sing a song. If you'd like to hear it, I can sing it for you".

2030 – When Computers become Human

Kubrick encouraged people to explore their own interpretations of the film and refused to explain "what really happened" in the movie, preferring instead to let audiences embrace their own ideas and theories.

2030 – When Computers become Human

"HER"

Compare the humanization of HAL in *2001: A Space Odyssey* (1968) with Samantha in "**Her**" (2013).

Spike Jonze's soulful sci-fi drama "**Her**" is about Theodore Twombly *(played by Joaquin Phoenix)*, a loner who works as a writer of computer-generated handwritten letters for clients.

Theodore purchases a new state-of-the-art computer with the ability to learn and grow with the user. He falls in love with his computer's highly advanced operating system with built-in artificial intelligence featuring the beautiful voice of Scarlett Johansson, but with no image of her. Instead, the viewer sees Samantha as:

2030 – When Computers become Human

Meanwhile, reluctant to sign the papers that will finalize his divorce from his childhood sweetheart, a depressed Theodore has slowly withdrawn from his supportive social circle, which includes his longtime friend Amy *(played by Amy Adams),* herself floundering in a failed marriage.

Adopting the name Samantha, the perceptive and emotional "software" gradually brings Theodore out of his shell. Soon, their relationship becomes intimate.

Their contributions to the relationship are mutual. Theodore teaches Samantha what it means to feel human, while Samantha gives him the strength to walk away from his failed marriage.

However, the relationship soon becomes conflicted and complicated when Samantha's rapidly accumulating knowledge base begins to alter the very core of their relationship, and Theodore learns that Samantha has many other relationships.

Some reviewers view this movie as artificial intelligence with a romantic lead. It is somewhat futuristic in that the Los Angeles where it is set has subways and trains that have supplanted the automobile and is sprawling with skyscrapers.

2030 – When Computers become Human

The movie projects a "green" society where most of the world's social and climatic maladies have been reduced or eliminated.

What comes through is Samantha herself, a complex, mature, and full-bodied character without a body. **"Her"** explores intimacy between two seemingly human characters, yet only one is human. So much is left to the viewer's imagination, yet nothing is lost in the viewer's delight.

The uplifting message from this movie is that a Samantha in the near future may be employed to bring troubled, lonesome introverts out of isolation and into a world of interactive sociability.

People suffering from social anxiety may feel more comfortable interacting with an intuitive system that understands them without their being uncomfortable.

Autonomous Computing

Tremendous advances have been made in the past decade in autonomous computing. An autonomous computing system is a system with sensory input that mimics human senses[15], a knowledge base, a dedicated purpose *(its operating system),* and responses *(effectors)* as output.

A generic schematic of an autonomous machine, regardless of its purpose, looks like this:

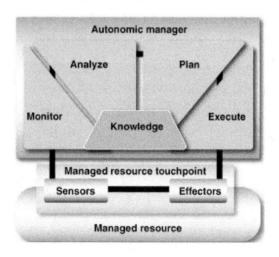

---

[15] The least of which is taste.

2030 – When Computers become Human

Autonomous systems are:

- ➤ Self-managing - the system monitors itself.

- ➤ Self-configuring - they reconfigure themselves automatically.

- ➤ Self-optimized - Complex middleware sets their own tunable parameters.

- ➤ Self-improving – they seek ways to improve their operations.

- ➤ Self-healing – They identify the root cause of their failures and are adaptive.

- ➤ Self-protected – they defend their system as a whole against large-scale problems arising from malicious attacks.

2030 – When Computers become Human

Autonomous systems are **not** Drones, which must be remotely controlled by a human being. Autonomous computers are self-managing and adapt to unpredictable changes while masking the intrinsic complexity that operates them. They are capable of building knowledge *(or policies)* based upon their environment, ultimately reducing barriers that existed in their initial launch.

As autonomous devices become more complex and capable, predictions in 2014 were that their number will grow by 40% each year. They will continue to be automatic, adaptive, and aware, but with increasing capability and purpose.

Self-driving Vehicles

WHO WAS FIRST?

At the 1939 New York World's Fair, General Motors exhibited the first "self-driving car" in its Futurama exhibit. Invented by Norman Bel Geddes, this was an electric vehicle propelled by electromagnetic fields that were generated from magnetized metal spikes embedded in a private experimental roadway. It was a very futuristic and streamlined design, as shown below:

2030 – When Computers become Human

WIRE-GUIDED VEHICLES

In 1953, RCA Laboratories created a miniature car which was guided and controlled by wires embedded in the lab's floor. This led to a project conceived by a traffic engineer in the Nebraska Department of Roads to experiment with a full-sized vehicle in an actual highway installation. It was conducted on a 400-foot section of a public highway *(Highway 2)* outside of Lincoln, Nebraska. Detector circuits embedded in the pavement synched up with lights along the edge of the road. The experiment was developed in collaboration with General Motors, who equipped two standard GM vehicles with cognitive devices that simulated steering, acceleration, and brake control.

OHIO STATE'S CONTROLLED HIGHWAYS

In 1960, OSU's Control Systems Laboratory developed a prototype of a driverless car which was activated by electronic transmitters embedded in the highway. Four states (Ohio, Massachusetts, New York, and California submitted bids for the construction. The bid was never awarded.

VISION-GUIDED VAN

In the 1980's, Mercedes-Benz designed a vision-guided robotic van which achieved a speed of 39 miles per hour on trafficless streets in Munich.

LIDAR — SAFETY TECHNOLOGY

LIDAR (Light Detection and Ranging) is remote sensing technology that employs light in the form of a pulsating laser to precisely measure variable distances. It is similar to Radar and Sonar, but it uses laser-generated light waves to detect how long the light takes to hit an object or surface and reflect back to its scanner.

By measuring distances not only in terms of travel time but also capturing wavelengths, the data captured can be used to produce digital 3-D images of the target. Originally developed to produce high-resolution maps, it is now used for control and navigation for some autonomous vehicles.

There is controversy over whether LIDAR makes self-driving vehicles safer. By mapping the objects and surfaces surrounding the vehicle at the speed of light, Advanced Driver Assistance Systems (ADAS) can visualize the ever-changing environment around the vehicle and react to it.

2030 – When Computers become Human

LIDAR can be used to slow or speed up automobiles on autopilot in order to brake when it is too close to the vehicle in front of it or speed up in a lane to "go with the flow". It is also technology for keeping a vehicle within a lane on a divided highway.

The argument against using LIDAR in self-driving vehicles is that drivers, particularly in the Tesla, become too relaxed or distracted, feeling that their vehicle is truly on autopilot when in fact driver intervention may be required when an object is not recognized, or the vehicle does not respond to its environment due to shortcomings in LIDAR technology.

THE GOOGLE SELF-DRIVING VEHICLE

The first autonomous self-driving vehicle was probably Google's. This vehicle integrated GPS guidance, Google Maps and Google Street View to enhance the vehicle's capability and ensure passenger safety.

Google's cars on freeways tend to leave a shorter distance between themselves and the vehicles they follow than some driver-training manuals recommend, to discourage other motorists from darting dangerously into the space. And when its their turn to proceed at a four-way stop, Google's cars inch forward decisively so other drivers do not try to beat them through the intersection.

2030 – When Computers become Human

Driverless cars have been a dream for decades, largely as a way to reduce the carnage on the roads. About 35,000 people die of crashes in the U.S. annually, with 90 percent of the accidents due to human error, according to the National Safety Council. Google believes its autos could avoid many such mistakes.

Many experts believe the vehicles could be bunched together without risk of colliding, reducing traffic congestion and boosting productivity.

It is predicted that, by 2035, 75 percent of vehicles sold worldwide will have some autonomous capabilities, such as being able to park themselves or drive at least part of a trip on autopilot.

Getting these vehicles to the point where they need no human intervention will be a major challenge. It is unclear who would be liable if a self-driving car caused an accident. pany co-founder Sergey Brin has predicted that the Google self-driving vehicle could be commercially available as early as 2017. However, their use would probably be restricted to limited areas for ridesharing services or others who could operate the cars more economically.

True North - The Brain on a Chip

In August 2014, IBM announced that its **Almaden Research Center** in San Jose, California had delivered its **True-North SyNAPSE** chip, a programmable "neurosynaptic" computer chip, the size of a postage stamp, with 5.4 billion transistors, one million programmable neurons, 256 million programmable synapses, and capable of 46 billion "synaptic" operations per second per watt.

IBM's comparison of the chip in traditional computers with neurosynaptic chips reveals:

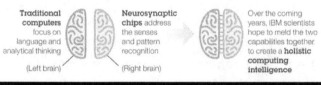

image via IBM.

This technology is now transforming science, technology, business, government, and society. The IBM team envisions a world populated with sensors that could process data at the speed of the human brain.

2030 – When Computers become Human

The result is architecture on silicon that mimics the human brain. It was funded by a $53.5 million research grant from DARPA. Like the brain, the SyNAPSE is event-driven and enables vision, auditory, and other multi-sensory applications.

The "brain on a chip" operates in biological real time, while consuming a minuscule 70mW, an order of magnitude that consumes less power than a modern microprocessor. Running on the energy equivalent of a hearing-aid battery, this technology could transform science, technology, business, government, and society, especially when it converges with 5g speed on devices.

It is expected that, when imbedded in drones, the SyNAPSE will result in a more refined perception of the environment, bringing cognitive computers to society. The end-result is low-power computing that solves problems in sensing and movement, something that digital computers do awkwardly. The team did emphasize that they are not aiming to create an artificial brain, which they feel is impossible.

2030 – When Computers become Human

IBM's team member Dharmendra Modha, co-author of a study outlining the chip's development, describes it as "a new machine for a new era." He believes that they can now design a computer that is as efficient as the human brain. **True North** diverts from traditional "von Neumann" digital computer architecture and more closely mimics the brain's neural functions by having a core driven only when an electrical charge reaches a specific value.

The future use of this chip is limitless. It is ideal for facial recognition. It has incredible potential and could be used in eyeglasses for the visually impaired, implanted in the ears of the partially deaf or the eyes of the partially blind, and used in medical imaging to detect early signs of disease. It can certainly improve the capabilities of driverless vehicles.

Wearable Devices

As processors become faster with 5g speed widely available, a proliferation of portable devices for consumers will expand dramatically into the marketplace, where many devices will not be carried, but worn instead.

THE APPLE WATCH

A groundbreaking announcement by Scott Cook, Apple's CEO at their September 2014 iPhone 6 event was the introduction of the **Apple Watch**[16]. The Apple Watch is now *(in 2020)* Apple's best-selling product.

APPLE WATCH ORIGINAL DESIGN FEATURES

[16] Surprisingly, it is not called the Apple iWatch!

2030 – When Computers become Human

- ❖ Communication

- ❖ Digital Touch. Users can draw quick images and send them to their friends.

- ❖ Emoji. Similar to emoticons on your phone, but these can be customized and animated.

- ❖ Receive Calls and Text. Its compatible with the iPhone 5 and beyond. When text is received, it is analyzed, and the watch responds by suggesting replies.

- ❖ Walkie-talkie. Used to send short voice messages, it is probably far advanced from Dick Tracy's 2-Way Wrist Radio of 1946.

- ❖ Wi-Fi. Built in to communicate with the iPhone.

FITNESS DEVICES FEATURES

❖ Measure heart rate.

❖ Accelerometer.   Counts   your   steps, calculates calories burned, and measures total body activity.

App development. A tool called the WatchKit is available for developers who create third-party apps.

iTunes and Apple TV access. Listen to iTunes radio.

Siri. On the watch, it integrates with the Maps feature to provide guided directions.

Apple Pay. A virtual wallet that digitizes and encrypts bank transactions.

2030 – When Computers become Human

The Computer Becomes Human

When does a computer *really* become human? As Turing suggested in his **Imitation Game**, it is probably when a computer or device cannot be distinguishable from a human *(at least if they are not seen)*.

The most important characteristic of a computer that is indistinguishable from a human are:

> **Emotional Detection** – detects happiness, sadness, anger, fear, surprise, and disgust.

> **Sensory Capability** – It is "aware" and can receive stimuli from sensors that "effect" actions or responses.

It is not necessary that the humanized computer have a processor such as the True North chip that simulates the brain. However, emotions and sensors are not likely to be present on a PC's typical processor.

How will advances in technology produce computers with emotions? Scientists and researchers are making advances in emotional artificial intelligence, which is also called affective computing.

125 | P a g e

2030 – When Computers become Human

Researchers have developed facial recognition software that can recognize emotions in students such as frustration, confusion, or boredom, and use these observations to improve the quality of education and educators.

Google's Futurist in Chief, Ray Kurzweil, is involved with *semantic search*, where advanced search algorithms can "understand" the context and intentions of a query, which can result in a conversation between the user and her computer.

Kurzweil said "I've had a consistent date of 2029 for that vision. And that doesn't just mean logical intelligence. It means emotional intelligence, being funny, getting the joke, being sexy, being loving, understanding human emotion. That's actually the most complex thing we do. That is what separates computers and humans today. I believe that gap will close by 2029."

There are parallel developments in this area of research. **Affectiva** has developed facial recognition software that analyzes expressions and physiological responses to detect human feelings.

2030 – When Computers become Human

An Israeli company, **Beyond Verbal**, determines emotions based upon human sounds and tone of voice. Microsoft's **Kinect** tracks players' heartbeats and physical movements when playing games to gain insight about how people feel when they play those games.

Humanoid robots, like the **Nao** not only react to emotions, but learn to imitate them.

Scientists at MIT have constructed a robot with a synthetic head and movable eyelids, eyes and lips. Parents are invited to play with **Kismet**, who initially looks sad, but smiles when it detects a human face. If the parent moves too fast, Kismet expresses fear.

ABOUT THE AUTHOR

After graduating from the U.S. Coast Guard Academy with a degree in Marine Engineering, Pete served as an officer on several assignments in the Pacific and in California. During his six years in the Coast Guard, he was Commanding Officer of two Coast Guard units

His information technology career includes systems design and development positions at IBM, EDS, and Chevron. Pete served in project management roles designing, developing, and managing major financial systems projects at Chevron and Household Financial Services.

Presently, Pete provides business consulting services to businesses, large and small, in many industries. His focus is in integrating his clients' business applications seamlessly with company web sites and other installed business applications. Many of Pete's clients are wineries, manufacturers, or distributors.

Pete has been intimately involved with his Coast Guard Academy class of 1961 and has published **"Sixty-one Never Outdone"** in 2020, available as a paperback or eBook on Amazon Books *(Kindle Direct Press)*.

2030 – When Computers become Human